MW01241045

Wealth Beyond Taxes

*How Healthcare Professionals Are Using The Tax
Code To Their Advantage To Generate More Income
and Wealth*

Joseph Yocavitch

DISCLAIMER:
This book contains the opinions and ideas of the author. The purpose of this book is to provide you with helpful information about financial planning. Careful attention has been paid to ensure the accuracy of the information, but the author cannot assume responsibility for the validity or consequences of its use. The material in this book is for informational purposes only. As each individual situation is unique, the author disclaims responsibility for any adverse effects that may result from the use or application of the information contained in this book. Any use of the information found in this book is the sole responsibility of the reader.

CONTENTS

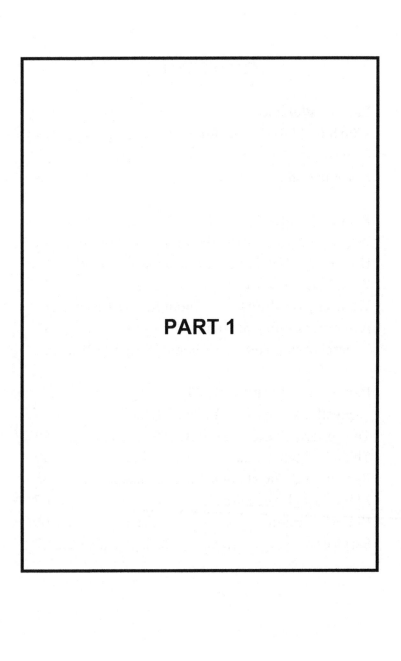

PART 1

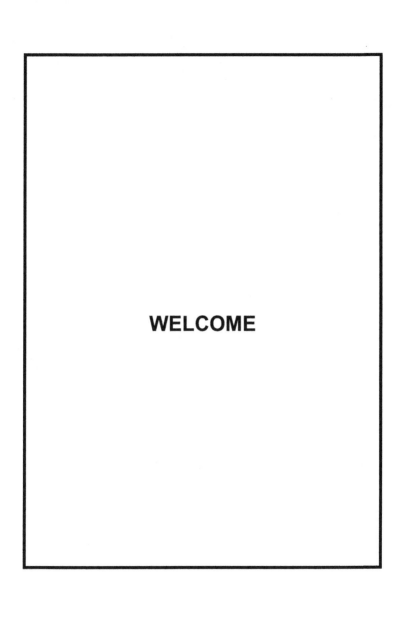

WELCOME

WHO SHOULD READ THIS BOOK?

There are two things I want you to know about me right from the start. The first is that as of the day I am writing this, my experience in helping individuals and families with their financial planning is 37 years. I hold the Life Underwriting Training Council Fellow (LUTCF®), Certification in Long-Term Care (CLTC®), Certified College Planning (CCPS), and a Registered Investment Advisor. I am also a John Maxwell certified trainer, coach, and team member.

The question that I typically get asked as well is, "*Are you a fiduciary?*" And the answer is yes. If you are not already familiar with the term fiduciary, let me give you the Reader's Digest version of what that means. I must by law put my clients' interests ahead of my own.

The second thing I'd like you to know about me is that over the past 37 years I have worked with a variety of people from all walks of life. But increasingly I discovered that some of my best clients and people that I most enjoy working with are doctors, nurses, and other business owners and professionals in the healthcare industry.

While healthcare professionals may share similar goals and aspirations to folks in other industries, there are specific characteristics of your industry that I have gotten to know intimately. I have become an expert in helping professionals just like you take advantage of all of the options that are available when it comes to using the tax code to pay less in tax, legally, ethically, and morally.

If you are a healthcare professional (a W2 employee, 1099 contractor, or business owner) the Wealth Beyond Taxes strategies outlined in this book can help you pay significantly less in taxes over the course of your lifetime and help you generate more income and wealth for you and your family.

MY PROMISE TO YOU

If you are still with me, I promise not to waste the next hour or so of your life. Quite the contrary, and I truly hope this book gives you a new option and inspiration when it comes to planning for both your present-day finances and your future retirement.

If you picked up this book then I think I know a few things about you already.

1. **You're not stupid.** Your financial picture may not be as solid as you want it to be, but not because you didn't pay attention. You listened to the experts and did what they advised you to do. You probably consult a financial advisor now, have a CPA do your taxes, and follow the trends in the market.

2. **You're not lazy.** You work hard and earn every penny that comes your way. By working hard and using your talents, you earn a good living. You will do almost anything it takes to provide for your family and secure their future. I applaud you!

3. **You're not looking for a magic bullet**. Okay, it would be nice if there were some genie in a bottle to grant you the financial well-being you want. (If you find one, feel free to give me a call.) But you're not counting on it or even looking for it. You want the facts and can make up your own mind when presented with those facts.

Anybody who knows me knows I tend to be direct, matter of fact, and detest wasting time (*which is why this book is designed to be read from cover to cover in less than 1 hour.*)

I promise to do my part and give you proven and effective strategies to significantly reduce the amount of taxes you'll pay to the government over the course of your lifetime.

INTRODUCTION

You're probably like most people who want a life filled with happiness, adventure, and opportunity. We all want to enjoy our retirement years surrounded by those we love and doing the things we enjoy. And during the journey toward retirement, we also want peace of mind knowing we're on the right path.

I'll also bet you've complained about taxes at some point during the last 12 months. *"So, what can I do about it?"* you ask yourself. You already work with a team of trusted advisors who help you prepare and pay your taxes each year, right?

Here's the problem with most CPAs when it comes to taxes. They focus all their time on recording the history their clients give them. They put the right numbers in the right boxes on the right forms and get them filed by the right deadlines.

By the time your income tax deadline rolls around each year there isn't much they can tell you other than to put more into your tax-deferred retirement accounts like a 401(k) or IRA.

On the surface, this may sound like sage advice. You'll pay less taxes this year than you would have otherwise, right? (More about this in Chapter 1.)

Have you ever heard of "the law of hammer?" The law of the hammer is a cognitive bias that involves an over-reliance on a familiar tool. As Abraham Maslow said in 1966, *I suppose it is tempting, if the only tool you have is a hammer, to treat everything as if it were a nail."*

If this is the advice you are getting from your CPA then you may very well have a tax storm gathering.

Stock market risk and burdensome taxes during retirement have created a retirement crisis that has affected the majority of Americans and has probably affected those close to you.

Forbes tells us that we're on the precipice of the greatest retirement crisis in the history of the world. In the decades to come, we will witness millions of elderly Americans, the Baby Boomers, and others, slipping into poverty. Too frail to work, too poor to retire will become the "new normal" for many elderly Americans.

So, you're probably wondering, "Okay, Joe, you've painted the picture. How do I avoid this doomsday scenario with my taxes and future retirement?"

That's a great question and I'm glad you asked. Let's dive into it.

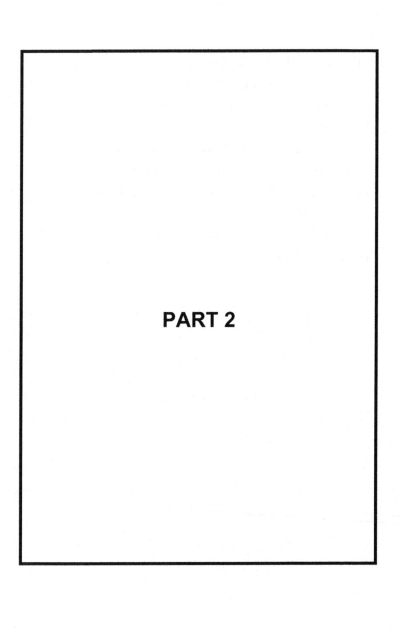

PART 2

WEALTH BEYOND TAXES

Chapter 1

WHY ISN'T MY CPA ALREADY DOING THIS FOR ME?

In today's world, most financially successful healthcare professionals and business owners simply assume that their CPA will bring them innovative tax planning ideas when appropriate to their situation. But that is simply not the case. Traditional CPA firms are asked to do so much and are stretched too thin just trying to produce a compliant tax return or financial statement.

Many CPAs are inundated with smaller clients who generate very little revenue for them and take up a lot of resources. They focus all their time on recording the history a client gives them and putting the right numbers in the right boxes on the right forms and getting that client's tax returns filed by the right deadlines.

11

But then they call it a day and move on to the next return. By that point, there's not much they can do to change that history (other than encouraging that client to make an occasional 401(k) contribution). So, they don't even try to change it before moving on to the next return.

It's like driving a car using a rear-view mirror instead of looking up the road. You would never try and back your car out of the garage, back it down the driveway to the street, and back it all the way to work, would you?

But this is the reality of why your CPA typically won't bring you any fresh ideas other than to add more money to your 401(k) or other tax-deferred retirement accounts.

Now, recording history is important, and it's important to do it right. You -- (along with the IRS!) -- want to know how much you make in a year.

But once you hit a certain level of income and taxes, you move beyond wanting to know just how much you owe. **You increasingly want to know how to pay less in taxes.** Unfortunately, most accountants aren't giving that information to you, nor should they, since it really isn't what they do. As we discussed above, their main function is to record your financial history and provide that information to the government.

The reality is that the US Tax code is one of the world's most complicated legal documents with over 150,000 pages and counting. Nobody seems to know how many pages are actually in the current tax code, as it is constantly changing, growing, and becoming more complex.

Now to be fair, CPAs don't spend all their time simply recording history. Plenty of them create year-end projections for their clients. This involves sitting down with a calculator and income statement, estimating how much the client will owe based on the best estimate of those numbers, and adjusting the client's January 15 estimated tax payments up or down based on how those numbers look.

They call that "planning" because it helps clients plan for a bigger or smaller tax bill. And there's real value in planning to avoid an ugly April 15th surprise. But this sort of process isn't really planning at all -- it's projection. The CPAs who do this for their clients are just projecting more scenarios to determine how much the client will eventually owe. And they generally complete the entire exercise without even considering ways to reduce that new, more accurate number.

When you press your CPA for more proactive ways to pay less, this is where they will normally tell you that you should put more money toward your retirement plan -- after all, it will defer the taxes you owe on the money thereby allowing you to pay less taxes immediately. Problem solved, right?

Chapter 2

HOW YOUR 401(K) COULD
BE A TICKING TAX BOMB

When planning for retirement, the options often discussed are likely familiar: 401(k)s and individual retirement arrangements, known as IRAs.

When information is detailed or hard to process, it's human nature to gravitate toward what we know, and these two savings vehicles are the ones most of us have heard of.

But what is a 401(k) or an IRA? What is a 403(b) or TSP?

These are simply tax codes.

Once we understand that a 401(k) and the like are simply a tool that we can use in saving our money, we then need to understand the tax implications of that tool.

Albert Einstein is quoted as saying that **one of the most complex things in the world is the**

United States Internal Revenue Code. So, if that's true, then what we have to understand is that the things we put inside of these tax codes - investments, mutual funds, ETFs[1], stocks, bonds, real estate, gold, precious metals[2], Bitcoin, etc. -- these things are ALL subject to taxation depending on the environment in which they are saved.

Retirement plans like 401(k)s, IRAs, and other government plans are designed to postpone the taxes you pay on your earned income. If you are in a higher tax bracket today then when you take it out, you will save money on taxes (you win). If, on the other hand, you are in a lower tax bracket today then when you take it out, you'll pay more taxes (you lose).

If we put our savings into an investment vehicle that defers taxes, we may be very likely hurting ourselves. Why? **Because the U.S. government believes in compound interest as well.**

That is, would you rather pay taxes on the seed (the amount you put in) or on the harvest (the amount you are taking out).

So, the important question becomes whether or not to postpone when you pay taxes.

The truth is, it's easy to answer that question because the evidence is overwhelming. Most people are clearly retiring in higher tax brackets than in their working years. **They are losing the tax game.**

In the late '70s and '80s when retirement plans like the 401(k) started being used, tax brackets were extremely high and were designed to be lower in retirement years. **The tax postponement strategy that worked then is simply not working today.**

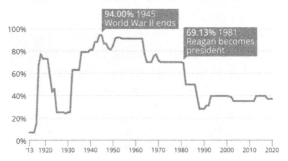

Taxing The Rich: How America's Marginal Tax Rate Evolved

Historic highest marginal income tax rates in the U.S.˙

94.00% 1945
World War II ends

69.13% 1981
Reagan becomes president

100%
80%
60%
40%
20%
0%
'13 1920 1930 1940 1950 1960 1970 1980 1990 2000 2010 2020

* Marginal tax rate is the highest tax rate paid on someone's income and only applies to income over a certain level. - e.g. earnings above $200,000 in 1960 were taxed at 90%.
Source: Tax Policy Center

statista

The majority of Americans are socking money into retirement plans that postpone taxes, which is a poor bet. Across the board, people are retiring with more income and/or lower deductions, and it's truly killing their retirement income.

When you contribute money to a tax-deferred account, it's a bit like going into a business partnership with the IRS. The problem is, every year the IRS gets to vote on what percentage of your profits they get to keep.

So, I have a question for you...

In the future, do you believe taxes will go up, go down or stay the same? We all might have our own opinion on that, but the Congressional Budget Office has already answered that question for us. **Not only do they say taxes must go up, but they must go up substantially.**

They did a study based on the government's current debt situation, which concluded that with no changes to Social Security, Medicare, and Medicaid, the lowest tax bracket would have to increase by two and a half times in order to sustain those programs.

Here's the really bad news. They also said that the 25% bracket would rise to 63% and the highest bracket, 39.6% would need to rise to 88%. Can you imagine 88% of your nest egg going to the IRS in taxes? That's a risk I'm not willing to take with my life savings.

[2]Investments in commodities may have greater volatility than investments in traditional securities, particularly if the instruments involve leverage. The value of commodity-linked derivative instruments may be affected by changes in overall market movements, commodity index volatility, changes in interest rates or factors affecting a particular industry or commodity, such as drought, floods, weather, livestock disease, embargoes, tariffs and international economic, political and regulatory developments. Use of leveraged commodity-linked derivatives creates an opportunity for increased return but, at the same time, creates the possibility for greater loss.

Chapter 3

WHAT MATTERS MOST TO YOU?

As we discussed in Chapter 1 *Why Isn't My CPA Already Doing This For Me?* you are likely being advised by your CPA that the way to pay less tax (this year!) is to put more money in your tax-deferred retirement accounts.

And as we discussed in Chapter 2 *How Your 401(k) Could Be a Ticking Tax Bomb*, you are already likely working with an advisor or money manager who is tasked with getting you the best rate of return for your stock portfolio inside of your tax-deferred accounts like your 401(k) or IRA.

Nothing wrong with that. That is very typical for most people.

One of the things that I've learned in my career is that there are rules that financial institutions such as banks typically know, but most regular investors don't.

The way I like to illustrate this is, "Have you ever played a game of tic-tac-toe?"

Who won the game the first time you played it? Most likely, the person who introduced you to the game. The person who showed you how to play the game.

"You want to play tic-tac-toe, three in a row?" They likely won.

Your CPA, while likely an excellent accountant and a nice person, and someone who you should trust when it comes to filing your yearly tax returns and paying your quarterly estimates, is likely not the best person to get advice from on how to significantly pay less taxes over the course of your lifetime.

Likewise, your money manager is likely not a retirement-income specialist. Instead, he is likely narrowly focused on managing your money, keeping your focus on average rates of return your portfolio is earning. It's not his role to show you how to maximize your income in retirement. He just wants to help you climb to the top of the mountain.

But retirement is not about just getting to the top of the mountain. It's about getting back down the mountain or living until the end of your life without having to sacrifice your lifestyle out of uncertainty and fear.

So, what else should you be thinking about when it comes to planning for retirement?

Everyone is different, and your goals are uniquely your own. So, when it comes to defining goals, here are the six most common priorities people have.

Income, a.k.a. cash flow, a.k.a money you can spend. This means that when you go into retirement your role has changed from that of an accumulator to that of a spender, and the purpose of your wealth is to provide you with income/cash flow that you can spend. It is not a reflection or commentary on the type of investor personality you may associate with (i.e., Safety/ Income/ Growth/ Aggressive Growth). It merely indicates that Income of some amount is a requirement from your accumulated wealth in order to meet your spending needs that are not covered by Social Security, pension, or other sources.

Growth is a priority whereby you ensure that the focus of your portfolio is to appreciate in value, understanding that with potential growth comes the potential risk of loss. In my experience, many times the person will want to and be willing to dial down the market risk in their portfolio and from the overall planning perspective generally. The reason many people include Growth in their priorities in retirement is to enable their income to keep pace with inflation. Alternatively, for funds not needed for their own retirement income, investing them for growth may result in more money left for the beneficiaries and thus be a legacy motivation.

Preservation means *"Don't lose my money!"*. Or, as Will Rogers once said, *"I am more concerned with the return of my money than a return on my money"*. For purposes of our discussion, it means that to some degree a person is not willing to accept a loss in exchange for a higher rate of return. The person for whom preservation is a priority will focus more of their plan on guaranteed principal assets. Preservation does not have to be absolute. Frequently, the plan designed with a client will result in x% of the assets being protected from investment risk.

Liquidity. That sum of money which is easily accessible by you, at a moment's notice. Most of the time, people think of this as cash in the bank, but it could be "stored" in other types of accounts as well. The point is that a specific sum of cash is readily accessible. For some people, this number is reflective of a certain number of months of household operating cash flow. For others, it includes a reserve for maintenance and repairs on the house, like hot water heaters, a/c systems, etc.

Heirs & Beneficiaries. As the name implies, H & B refers to the financial and other resource benefits you wish to leave for other people you love when you die. For families with young children, Heirs and Beneficiaries is much higher on the list. For older clients, Heirs & Beneficiaries will typically be lower on the list. For older clients with special-needs children and/or those whose objectives include legacy for children or grandchildren, H&B would be higher on the list. Almost always, those with wealth in excess of what they will spend in their own lifetimes seek to maximize what stays in the family.

Debt. In addition to taxes, debt is one of the biggest destroyers of wealth. From a planning perspective, figuring out how to eliminate personal debt quickly will greatly accelerate the wealth-creation process.

Chapter 4

WHAT THE WEALTHY KNOW ABOUT RISK AND TAXES

Warren Buffet, one of the greatest investors of our day, subscribes to the following philosophy when it comes to investing.

"Rule number one is to never lose money. Rule number two is to never forget rule number one."

I agree! And if you do too, then you'll love what you are about to learn in this chapter.

Let's take a brief journey back in time...

In October 1929, the stock market suffered severe losses. It plunged over 22% in just a few short days, making headlines across the country. Over the next several years, the markets would have difficulty recovering. The Dow Jones Industrial Average[1] would take a staggering 32-year setback, losing nearly 90% of its value.

From its peak of 381.17 in September 1929, it would close at a shocking 41.22 on July 8, 1932. It would take another 22 years to surpass its all-time high before the crash of 1929.

During that period of time:

Nearly 25% of all Americans would be unemployed and unable to find work.

Over 40% of banks would shut down.

Millions of savings accounts would simply disappear.

But in the midst of all that devastation, there was a silver lining for some people.

Life insurance companies remained virtually unaffected during that tumultuous time. More importantly, while the market suffered severe losses, **the policy owners of cash value life insurance didn't lose a dime!**

That's such an important point, let me say it again.

During the Great Depression, arguably one of the worst periods of economic disaster our country has ever been through, those who had invested in cash value life insurance policies didn't lose a dime!

In fact, cash value life insurance was such a stable place to have money that while many people lost everything those who owned cash value life insurance were even paid profits in every single year of the Great Depression![2]

Fast forward to our present time. With out-of-control government spending and debt and our world being radically reshaped both politically and economically as a result of the coronavirus pandemic, knowing how and where to keep your money safe (and out of reach of the IRS!) is becoming increasingly important.

Banks and Corporations

While many wealthy individuals maximize the use of cash value life insurance, there is one specific group that really understands its value. This same sector of the economy controls nearly every aspect of our economy.

Cash-value life insurance plays a massive role in financial institutions, corporations, and banks. These organizations buy life insurance by the billions, and use it for many different reasons. In fact, banks have as one of their top tier one assets cash value life insurance almost twice as much as real estate.

Not only does it increase their financial stability and reduce their taxes, but it is also an ideal place to fund employee pensions, healthcare costs, and other benefits.

The FDIC makes available the balance sheets of nearly every major bank. The following figures are directly from FDIC.gov and represent the exact amount of money the following banks hold in life insurance.

Bank	Life Insurance Assets
Bank of America	$19,607,000,000
Wells Fargo Bank	$17,739,000,000
JP Morgan Chase Bank	$10,327,000,000
U.S. Bank	$5,451,892,000

Banks are in the business of money. They have some of the greatest minds in the world, including economists, attorneys, accountants, financial analysts, and other experts helping them increase the efficiency and use of their capital.

It is not insignificant that banks place billions of dollars in life insurance. It's a reflection of the value they place on this powerful asset. For banks, it provides the ultimate in safety, stability, and growth.

Corporations are also heavily involved in investing heavily in cash value life insurance. It is also significant to note that these corporations rely heavily on life insurance to fund an employee's retirement plan and their top executives' retirement plans.

Among its many benefits, the ability of cash value life insurance to provide the stable growth necessary to create a predictable income is one of its most powerful features.

Here is a list of some well-known companies that hold cash value life insurance as an asset[3]:

- Starbucks
- Johnson & Johnson
- Pfizer
- Verizon
- Comcast
- Walt Disney
- Lockheed Martin

- Nike
- CVS
- Bed, Bath & Beyond
- General Electric

In the 1900s, it's estimated that over 50% of savings went into cash value life insurance.[4] It was the staple for safety, protection, and predictable future income for decades.

Today, Americans are being told by Wall Street and others with vested interests that volatile, risk-based investing in the stock market is the best way to prepare for retirement.

"Why would they do that?" you may be asking. You see, Wall Street investment firms were a big part of how government plans like 401(k)s got established in the first place. These elite insiders positioned themselves to be the managers of the funds that ultimately made their way into these plans. There have been many books that go into much greater detail about this phenomenon. Suffice it to say here that there has been a massive transition for the worse from safety and guarantees to risky, unpredictable stock market investments.

Thousands of Americans are starting to see the outcomes of these failed models, and are looking for a better path.

---

[1] Indices are unmanaged and investors cannot invest directly in an index. Unless otherwise noted, performance of indices does not account for any fees, commissions, or other expenses that would be incurred. Returns do not include reinvested dividends.

The Dow Jones Industrial Average (DJIA) is a price-weighted average of 30 actively traded "blue chip" stocks, primarily industrials, but includes financials and other service-oriented companies. The components, which change from time to time, represent between 15% and 20% of the market value of NYSE stocks.

[2] Patch, B. W. (1933). Life insurance in the depression. *Editorial research reports 1933* (Vol. I).
http://library.cqpress.com/cqresearcher/cqresrre19330519 00

[3] Dyke, Barry James. "CORPORATE-OWNED LIFE INSURANCE." The Pirates of Manhattan: Systematically Plundering the American Consumer & How to Protect against it. Portsmouth, NH: 555 Publishing. 2007.174-176. Print.

[4]Thompson, Jake. "Money. Wealth. Life Insurance." Jake Thompson. 2013. 14. Print.

Chapter 5

A MORE TAX EFFICIENT SAVINGS STRATEGY

Cash value life insurance is one of the most tax-friendly financial tools we have. Money inside cash value life insurance, when handled properly, grows tax-free, can be used tax-free, and passes on tax-free.

"But I Can Get A Better Return In The Stock Market"

You might think the point of this section is to try and convince you that you can't get better returns, but it's not.

I strongly believe that conventional forms of investing -- especially stocks and mutual funds -- will fall far short of what a solid cash value policy will do with much less risk. And that's not even the most important aspect of cash value life insurance.

One of the most important benefits of cash value life insurance is your guaranteed access to your money at any time you want it. If you feel you can get better returns somewhere else, and you're willing to take the risk, the insurance policy will actually make the investment more profitable.

For example, imagine you have money in a life insurance policy. And also imagine you have an opportunity to go in on a time-sensitive real estate investment. You are convinced that this real estate investment will pay you DOUBLE-DIGIT returns consistently for a number of years to come. That's fantastic! You can easily access the money inside your cash value life insurance policy to fund the real estate investment.

Conversely, if you had your money tied up in a government retirement plan, you would likely not have been able to take advantage of this opportunity without being penalized and being taxed!

Tax-free growth

Among many benefits, I believe the most attractive benefit of cash value life insurance is the way it is taxed. This benefit alone attracts those that want protection from the uncertainty of taxes.

Let's talk about a few of those tax benefits.

The first, and arguably one of the most important, is tax-free growth.

How is this possible?

Growth inside of some insurance policies is called a dividend, and by definition, is considered a "return of premium." Since the IRS considers this a return of what you have already paid, it is not taxable. In other policies, growth is called a credit and because of tax codes 72e and 7702 no income tax is due when you access this cash value.

That being said, there is one caveat to this; as the policy grows, you will have undoubtedly accumulated more than you contributed if you've designed your policy for high cash value. If at any point you decide to withdraw your money from the insurance policy, the growth (everything above the cost basis of the policy) can be taxable.

However, as long as you keep the policy intact, **it will continue to grow tax-free indefinitely.** And as you'll soon discover, there is practically no reason to ever cancel the policy, keeping those dollars tax-free for the rest of your life.

The appeal of tax-free growth on your money is one of the biggest reasons large organizations and savvy individuals pump millions of dollars into these policies each year. You'll have a hard time finding a better place for these types of tax benefits.

Tax-free Death Benefit

When you've amassed a large amount of wealth over the course of your lifetime, there's only one thing that stands in the way of passing the benefit of that hard work on to your family...Uncle Sam!

In my view, the death tax is unfair, inefficient, economically unsound, and, frankly, immoral.

Whether you have a big estate or a small estate, passing on money can be painful. Some of the largest estates are stripped to nearly nothing after taxes and probate. It is estimated that the death tax causes one-third of all family-owned small businesses to liquidate after the death of the owner.

Would you like some good news?

In addition to the tax-free growth, which we outlined in the last section, cash value life insurance provides a tax-free death benefit to your loved ones.

This means your life insurance death benefit will transfer with no income tax to those you choose to leave it to.

I can assure you of one thing: there is no better asset to die with than life insurance. It is the most heavily used estate planning tool in the country because it can help pass on more of your hard-earned money to your family.

Chapter 6

SUPERCHARGING YOUR RETIREMENT WITH A LIRP

If you are between the ages of 45 to 65, you are likely more acutely aware of how well you have (or haven't!) saved for retirement.

To compensate, it may be helpful to avail yourself of another tool I oftentimes recommend to clients to use the tax code to their advantage to maximize their income and wealth, especially in retirement: the *Life Insurance Retirement Plan* (LIRP).

A LIRP is a life insurance policy that is specifically designed to maximize cash value accumulation. At the same time, it is designed to minimize the death benefit because the goal isn't the death benefit but the tax advantages it affords you while you are living.

If you recall from *Chapter 4 What the Wealthy Know About Risk*, corporations rely heavily on life insurance to fund an employee's retirement plan and their top executives' retirement plans. It should come as no surprise that about 85% of the CEOs of Fortune 500 companies utilize the LIRP as one of their primary retirement tools.

In addition to its tax-free benefits, the LIRP provides a compelling array of options for growing dollars within the tax-free accumulation account.

For example, you can do the following:

1. You can opt to grow your money within the general investment portfolio of the insurance company that administers the program. Because insurance companies are in the business of managing risk, these types of returns tend to be conservative, but very consistent.
2. You can pass your contributions through insurance companies into mutual fund portfolios called sub-accounts. While this approach can provide much higher returns,

it does expose you to the impact of market declines.

3. You can contribute dollars to an accumulation account whose growth is linked to the upward movement of a stock market index like the S&P 500.[1] You can participate in the growth of this index up to a cap, typically 11% and 13%. On the flip side, **if the index ever loses money, the account is credited zero so it actually never goes down in value.** With back-tested historical returns between 7% and 9%, this can be a safe but productive way to accumulate tax-free dollars for retirement.

One of my favorite features that some LIRPs can include is **leverage.**

Studies show that your retirement will likely cost you an average of 6 times more than your house. And if you are like most people, you have probably used financing to live in a better house than you would have otherwise been able to afford if you had to pay for the house in cash.

Similarly, Kaizen® is a life insurance tool that uses leverage and provides you an opportunity to earn significantly more interest while at the same time eliminating the risk of market decline.

What is revolutionary about Kaizen® is that it provides you the opportunity to add up to 3 times more money using other people's money.

As a result of this leverage, you have the potential for an additional 60-100% of tax-free income in retirement, and without the typical risks associated with leverage.

"Why Haven't I Ever Heard of Kaizen®?"

Historically, Kaizen, and other forms of LIRPs have been reserved for the wealthiest segment of America's population. It wasn't until recently that companies began to re-engineer these programs to mimic the Roth IRA. They knew if they could structure the LIRP to capture the tax-free qualities of the Roth IRA, **but without the accumulation limitations**, they would significantly benefit the everyday saver who was looking to maximize their tax-free income.

Is Kaizen the right strategy for you? As a fiduciary, I can't answer that question here. It depends on your unique circumstances and goals. If Kaizen does sound interesting to you, you can check out the following website so that you can learn more about it. https://www.myilia.com/kaizen Feel free to reach out to me with any questions about Kaizen. You can reach me at: jmlfinancialgroup@gmail.com

---

[1]The Standard & Poor's 500 (S&P 500) is an unmanaged group of securities considered to be representative of the stock market in general. It is a market value-weighted index with each stock's weight in the index proportionate to its market value.

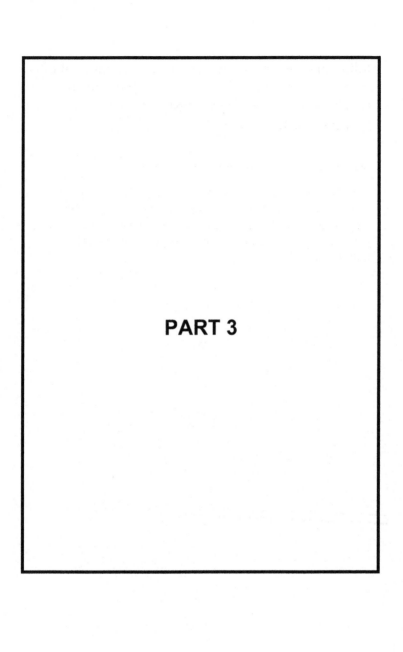

PART 3

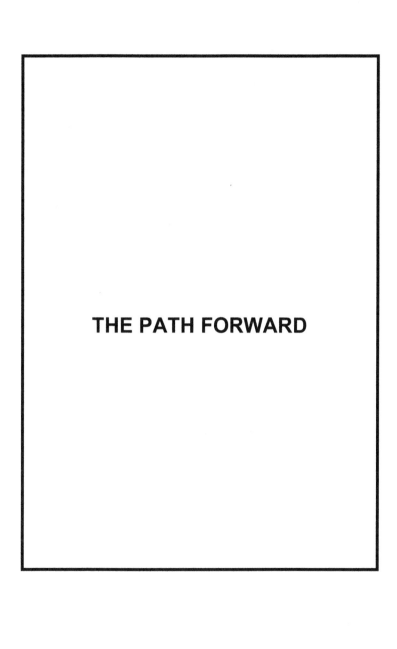

THE PATH FORWARD

7 QUESTIONS YOU NEED ANSWERED TO PROPERLY PLAN FOR RETIREMENT

This book, while intentionally small, is about big ideas. My goal has been to help you begin the exciting process of totally transforming the way you plan for your future retirement by leveraging the tax code to your advantage.

The #1 problem I've identified in my years as a financial planner is that dated strategies of maxing out 401(k)s or IRAs and utilizing a traditional 60/40 split for asset allocation[1] just isn't going to work anymore.

I don't want you to just REACH retirement, I want you to have enough income and wealth to thrive!

Toward that end, you should know the

answers to the following 7 questions... and if your advisor can't give them to you, you should fire them. Even if that advisor is you.

So, ask yourself, do you know the answers to these questions?

Do you know the rate of return you may need for you to live like you live today and have your money last?

My experience is that most people want to maintain their current lifestyle when they retire. Think of it like this: retiring could equate to being on unemployment...but for 30 years.

You've probably heard these 30 years referred to as 3 separate ten-year periods... "the go-go years," "the slow-go years," and "the no-go years." During these periods, having your money keep up with your desired lifestyle (including inflation), is not an easy feat.

You may have heard what I like to refer to as the "broken rule" from your human resource department or 401k, 403b, or TSP advisors –– "You only need 75% of your income in retirement." That advice is questionable. Your advisor or human resources representative never takes into account one of the greatest risks in retirement called "Sequence of Return Risk." In essence what that means is that if your existing retirement plan is using an average rate of return to forecast your probability of success, you may very well learn the hard way that averages lie.

Do you know how much you need to save each year to make sure you will have enough?

Quite simply, I show this figure to my clients last. The reason for that is because the answer is almost always depressing. I have learned that most folks will spend more time researching a 2-week vacation than they will learning about the nuances of retirement (also depressing, to some).

Retirement differs from when we are working because we turn off our income... that's it. No one can predict (*let alone wants to think about!*) when they will die. But if you're not planning for 30-40 years of retirement (and saving accordingly), you could find out in the later stages of life that a miscalculation can lead to an undesirable lifestyle.

For example, no one wants to pack up their most prized possessions and go to a nursing home. Put simply, nursing homes are depressing and carry the stigma that they are a place where you go to die. But what happens when someone exhausts all their resources and has not planned properly for an end-of-life event necessitating long-term care? The answer is devastating –- they could become a ward of the state and that's never pretty.

Do you know how long you will have to work before you can stop and have your money last to your life expectancy?

It's one thing being able to retire and work or consult at your leisure... but it's another thing to either HAVE to continue working or to be forced to STOP working due to an illness or disease.

I have seen folks retire after working their entire lives, only to have their health prevent them from living the golden years we all dream of.

Even worse, I have seen folks pass away too

soon, never expecting that they would become ill. Hug the ones you're with, make time for your family, and plan for the golden years to be just that: golden.

Too many financial advisors are narrowly focused on the rate of return of a portfolio instead of the quality of life that is desired.

Do you know how much you may need to reduce your future lifestyle to keep from running out of money?

This goes back to the 1st question and a myth that has circulated in the pre-retiree community for years. Why would someone want to live on 20-30% less than what they are living on now?

My job as a retirement income specialist is to help you maintain 100% of your current lifestyle while at the same time helping you safeguard that plan against unforeseen events. It's OK to make cutbacks in situations that call for it. But why intentionally design a 30% reduction in your lifestyle if you can avoid it?

Does your portfolio have cancer?

I know the "C" word is serious, ominous, and extreme. That is the reason I chose it. If you had cancer, would you want to know? I, for one, would, and I hope I never get it. It's an ugly disease.

Well, when your portfolio has cancer and no one has taken steps to eradicate it, you could find yourself with a lot less money than you had anticipated. What's this cancer called? Taxes!

I regularly speak with a lot of very educated individuals who you would think would have figured this out. But it's not intuitive.

What do I mean? Let me ask you these questions: Do you contribute to an IRA or 401K, 403b, or TSP (*these are all tax-deferred plans*)? I almost always get a 100% affirmation that they are not only participating in but investing as much as possible in these plans.

So, if this is true for you, the next question is this: Do you think income taxes in this country will be lower (as you were probably told initially) the same or higher when you retire? 100% of the folks I ask this question to answer, "Higher!"

I hate to break the news to you, but if you answered the same and think you can save money in a rising tax environment, this makes no mathematical sense.

To clarify, If I could have paid .25 cents on $1 today and possibly .33, .40, .50, or even .70 cents tax on that dollar in the future, you're making a HUGE miscalculation.

I understand folks do this because this is the advice everyone, including their CPAs and tax advisors and their human resources and employers are giving them...but the rules have changed and are changing very quickly still, and taking steps to eradicate this cancer is prudent.

Do you have a portfolio or a plan?

As a financial planner, I have learned not to idolize tools. Most people view their portfolios as the solution, when in fact it's just part of what they should be considering. It's not the fault of most people, though.

For years major insurance companies

and financial institutions have bombarded us with commercials with the message: "What's your number?" as folks walk around with this sum of money over their head. What a misleading commercial. Getting to retirement with a sum of money should not be the goal. Getting through retirement with enough assets, income, and desired lifestyle, would be a better strategy.

Retirement is not about how much money you have amassed, but instead, it's about identifying your income needs based on your specific criteria, and then figuring out if all of your assets will help generate enough supplemental income to meet your needs.

Remember this mantra: Retirement is about income, it's about income, it's about income.

What's your Sharpe Ratio?

Most people have never heard of Sharpe Ratio – and many don't know how it affects their portfolio. The formula for Sharpe Ratio is defined as the risk-free rate of return –- the average rate of return divided by standard deviation equals the Sharpe Ratio. In plain English, the formula for Sharpe Ratio answers the question "are you being rewarded enough for the amount of risk you are taking?"

Most folks have more risk in their portfolio than they know, and to make matters worse, they believe they are diversified[2], when in fact they are in investments like mutual funds and other holdings which quite often are identical across the board.

So now that you know the questions that you should be asking, what can you do right now to better prepare for the future? The answer is simple: get a second opinion.

If there are holes in your financial cruise ship, when do you want to be made aware? When it's still salvageable, or after the ship is taking on water and it's too far gone to save?

If you found that you didn't have the answers to the questions above, and you'd like help answering them, I want to invite you to take...

[1] Asset Allocation does not guarantee a profit or protect against a loss in a declining market. It is a method used to help manage investment risk.

[2] Diversification does not guarantee a profit or protect against a loss in a declining market. It is a method used to help manage investment risk.

Chapter 8

THE NEXT STEP

"It's not what you know; it's not even who you know; it's what you implement that counts."

Congratulations! You are one step closer to having the confidence that comes from knowing that you are on the right path to enjoying a retirement filled with happiness, adventure, and opportunity.

Imagine what it will feel like to know that both your future, that of your family, and your legacy are secure.

Trust me, it's gratifying and makes the entire planning process worthwhile.

As I said earlier, I wrote this book for two primary reasons: 1) to help, inform and motivate healthcare professionals like you; 2) to extend an invitation to see if working together to help you create more income and wealth makes sense -- for both of us.

If you like what you have read so far and feel that working directly with me to either create or improve your retirement plan makes sense, let me ask you to consider these three questions:

1. Do you believe taxes will go up in the future?
2. Are you serious and committed to using the tax code to your advantage legally, morally, and ethically, so that you and your family can create more income and wealth for years (*even generations!*) to come?
3. Do you value working with an expert to guide you, bring out the best in you, and prevent mistakes?

If your answers are three affirmations, then, as I see it, you have two pathways in front of you at this very moment in time.

1. You can close this book and do nothing with the information I shared. (If you have gotten this far, I surely hope this is not an option.)
2. You can schedule a 15-minute introductory phone call with me to begin the conversation on how we might work together.

If you are serious about your financial future, you have nothing to lose by choosing the second pathway.

This one phone call may hold the key to unlocking the door to your peace of mind knowing that you are on the right path to enjoying a retirement filled with happiness, adventure, and opportunity.

There is no obligation, and scheduling it is super easy.

I understand your goals are uniquely yours, which is why you and I need to talk -- if you are serious about implementing any of the ideas in this book.

This call is all about helping you decide if working together is a good fit for both of us. Maybe we are meant to work together. Maybe not. But we will not know unless you and I have this first, critical conversation.

Note: It's NOT a Sales Call

It's a two-way interview to make sure we agree this is a good match. I'll ask you some questions, and you can ask me some questions (in fact, as many questions as you want). And then, we can go from there.

This is typically a 15-minute phone call; however, we will stay on until you're satisfied you are ready to work with me or you simply want to move on. That's it. There is no obligation on your part.

I am a firm believer that everyone should be working with certain people -- not everybody -- but people who "get" you and understand what's most important to you and your family.

I feel the same way about the people whom I work with, and in order for us to see if we are a good fit, I have found these calls to be the ideal litmus test. It will give us a chance to "meet" and see if working together makes sense.

TODAY Is the Day. NOW Is the Time.

Schedule your **Wealth Beyond Taxes Strategy Session** with me right now. There's absolutely no fee, no obligation, no risk, and nothing to lose.

How to Schedule Our Call:

Go to https://jmlfinancialgroup.com/schedule and pick a day and time that works best for you. That's it! Or if you have any questions you can email me directly at: jmlfinancialgroup@gmail.com
I look forward to hearing from you, and more importantly, working together to help you create more income and wealth for you and your family for years to come!

RESOURCES & SOCIAL MEDIA

In addition to the resources I have already shared with you throughout this book here are a few more that you can check out.

My Website:
https://jmlfinancialgroup.com/

My LinkedIn:
https://www.linkedin.com/in/joseph-yocavitch-4023b513a/

TV Appearances:
https://jmlfinancialgroup.com/tv-appearances/

Podcast & Radio
https://jmlfinancialgroup.com/podcasts/

Other Books I've Written (*available on Amazon*):

"Getting Down The Mountain: How To Preserve Your Wealth from an Avalanche of Taxes and Other Threats"

"The Heart of Your Money: Inspiration for Financial Wellness"

ABOUT JOSEPH YOCAVITCH

Joe Yocavitch is the President and founder of JML Financial Group with more than 37 years of experience in the financial services industry. Over the course of his career, he has dedicated his focus to furnishing a wide range of services and products. Working with high-net-worth individuals, professionals, business owners, and retirees, he focuses on tax-efficient strategies, estate planning, business insurance, and investment strategies. Through his efforts and a reputation for outstanding service, he has built a solid client base and grown his business through referrals from clients.

Joe believes that commitment to excellence is a habit, not an act. He only recommends strategies that he himself would use. He also conducts seminars on various topics and is frequently invited to speak to groups on estate planning concepts. As a John Maxwell certified trainer, coach, and team member, he puts it this way:

I offer workshops, seminars, keynote speaking, and coaching to aid in personal and professional growth to individuals, organizations, and companies worldwide. My facilitated groups offer a combination of masterminding, peer brainstorming, education, accountability, and support in a group setting to sharpen your business and personal skills. By bringing fresh ideas and a different perspective, my professionals can help you achieve your goals.

Joe is a registered representative with Brokers International Financial Services, LLC, and is a graduate of the Life Underwriting Training Council. He holds a Bachelor of Arts in Business and Managerial Economics from the University of North Carolina at Chapel Hill.

Outside of the office, Joe enjoys golf, winemaking, fitness, and spending time with his family.

VIDEO INTERVIEW

I n addition, **I find that video is a great medium to get to know someone.**

Toward that end, I created this 17-minute video so you can get to know me a bit better and determine if you think we might be a good fit.

Here is the link to the 17-minute video.

https://go.smartfinancialhub.com/meetJoeYocavitch

I've included the transcript of the recording below for those who prefer to simply read.

Transcript

Question:

Who is Joe Yocavitch?

Joe Yocavitch:

I grew up in the Philadelphia area, Cherry Hill. I've always played sports my whole life in school, and I furthered my career in sports at school in North Carolina, and was lucky enough to have a tryout with the Kansas City Chiefs and signed on with them for a bit. Unfortunately getting hurt, caused my long-term career to be shortened, But I gained a few qualities; never to give up, tenacity, thinking out of the box, and always striving to win.

I took these traits into my financial planning practice. And because of that, I've been in the financial planning practice right now for going on 37 years. I have a securities license series 7[1], 63[2], and 65[3]. I have certifications in long-term care, retirement planning, investment advisory. I do work with a team of experts. including my wife. She's my business partner. We've been married for 34 years. I have two children, my son is following in my footsteps. So, I could not be any happier being able to have my son working with me and coordinating the things we do for our clients. And I'm having pretty much the best time of my life.

Question:

I'm aware of two other books that you've written, so you are a serial author. You're also a podcaster. Would you like to add anything about that?

Joe Yocavitch:

My company's called JML Financial Group, but we have a podcast called *The Heart Of Your Money*. I also have a radio show called *The Heart Of Your Money*. So, we're big believers in educating our clients, and I find that an educated client is a successful retirement client. They become better able to adapt on what I share with them. So, that, to me, is the most important thing. And to be able to coordinate with that and have a method that we talk to our clients about is fun. We work with a team of experts, CPAs, estate planning attorneys, property and casualty folks. We work with mortgage people and Medicare people. So, we're always in a team approach mode, when we're working with people.

We've actually come up with a couple of acronyms for that. We call it KASH, K is for Knowledge, today, you need to have a little different mindset when you're dealing with the things that are happening to us today. A is for attitude, we need to have an attitude change. We really need to get our head and heart together in alignment with each other. We also need to have good skills. The skills we acquire today, and ongoing, give us the advantages to be able to help people achieve things that they never would've ever managed to achieve. And then it's habits. We get a in a habit of doing things automatically with that mindset. And it's a philosophy that I have because we pretty much mentor our clients. We give them the necessary tools and the strategies to give them the maximum of all they want to do in life, in terms of money, lifestyle, and living a long, prosperous life in abundance mode.

Question:

You wrote this book specifically for healthcare professionals. What are some of the challenges that they're having? And, just tell us a bit more about your work with healthcare professionals.

Joe Yocavitch:

The healthcare professionals I work with, at times are unsure about where and how they should be saving their money. We're big believers of, it's more important where your wealth is located than what it earns. So, when we're working with health professionals, we help them understand all our philosophies in terms of how money works, how taxes work. And the biggest concern for us, Paul, now more than ever, where your money is invested so we have a three-bucket rule.

The first bucket is always tax money. This is the IRA, 401k, the 403(b), the 457 plans and so forth. Then we have the 2nd Bucket sometimes tax money, whereby some of the money is taxed differently. This is investments such as stocks and bonds and Real Estate. And then we have the 3rd Bucket, never taxed. This is where we have the tax-free municipal bonds. We have the ROTH IRAs, and we have the overfunded cash value life insurance.

And what we try to do with our clients is make sure they understand each bucket correctly. And most people, unfortunately, have been putting most of their emphasis on the first bucket, where they put all their money in the 401ks, the 403(b)s.

And we realize, they don't understand sometimes, that when they were doing it, it was a good thing. It was not a bad thing, because taxes were, at the time, pretty high.

But as you see, moving forward, taxes are changing. So, the strategy they did some years ago might not be as efficient moving forward into retirement. So, we want to make sure we share with them information, clearly strategies, not products, strategies that make the most amount of sense, but more importantly, to optimize every situation that comes down the road.

Question:

The book is called Wealth Beyond Taxes, and beyond what people should know about taxes, what are some of the other areas that you find that people need help with and where you're able to help them?

Joe Yocavitch:

What we find with the professionals out there, because I said earlier, most of their money is in 401k, that they're paying a high cost. They're paying high fees. Today, companies are now making the employees, the health professionals, be their own investment advisors. They have to understand risk. They understand cost, understand turnover and volatility. They have to have a lot of information just to understand how their money works. And because of tax efficiencies that we talk to our clients about, we need to have them understand when you're putting money away, is it more important in the present, or is it more important what that money's going to be like in the future and how it's going to be affected by taxes?

And more importantly, Paul, inflation. Now, inflation has been really running havoc across our country. So, the concern we have is to be able to look at things holistically. So, we do work with a number of our professional advisors, CPAs and attorneys and so forth, that help us help the client the best, most efficient way possible when it comes to these problems that we're all being faced with, moving forward in the future.

Question:

If someone already has CPA, money manager, et cetera, are they a good fit for what you do?

Joe Yocavitch:

The first time we meet with a client, we have what we call the family huddle. We get together and we huddle, and we discuss their situations with their current advisors, with their CPAs and attorneys. We ask them to share with us, almost like an x-ray of information. The second meeting we have is what we call a diagnostic review. We actually look at their current plan , from all the insurances and investments, and make sure what they think they have, they really do have. And then we go from there.

We then go into an offense and defensive strategy. And the offense is very simple. What is the best way to achieve the maximum amount of wealth with the individual? And the defensive ways, are what are tools you should be using to be able to defend yourself against the problems of death, disability, lawsuits, or living too long.

Now, that could be a good thing or a bad thing, but because of longevity, we have a much longer lifespan. We need to be able to have the right tools and the right strategies in place, to be able to live a long time, without these other exterior components hurting us, like taxes, like inflation, like volatility, like uncertainties. And now more than ever, we want to sit down with those people. And then from there, after we do our normal process with our client, we put a game plan together for them. We actually put a game plan together on the direction they should be taking. And then from there, we do an update of game-planning for them, once a year and continuously, to make sure the plan in place is maneuvering according to what we are faced with today. Because, being a health professional, we all know this, things are changing constantly in the marketplace. But we want to make sure our health professionals are in sync with how their money is aligning with their philosophy, and the best way to maximize their wealth and minimize taxes, if all possible.

Question:

What are some of the biggest misconceptions that people have about the work you do?

Joe Yocavitch:

Clients think we are all the same, and we're not. It's been my experience over my career of 37 years, people would get their license, and they would hang a shingle up and call themselves financial planners. And they would just sell products to you. at the end of the day, all you've collected is a bunch of products, almost like a junk drawer full of products.

Our approach is different. My early years were spent on Wall Street, with a big wire house. but I integrated with the insurance background. So, I have Strong insurance and investment knowledge to help my clients from all angles.

And when you combine those two things together, Paul, it becomes magical. And when you have a team approach with that, and you're really able to put both of those components together, because, remember, the Wall Street guys, all they want to do is put your assets under management, get a fee.

So they're not going to even talk to you about, putting any dollars into protection components, like disability insurance, like the right long-term care, or the right life insurance. They're going to have you continue to put money away and get a fee for that. And the other insurance folks, they'll continue to present just insurance vehicles to you.

But because of my background, I'm able to combine both of those together, which makes it unique, because I'm offering a very broad-brush approach and a holistic approach. We'll be able to help people look at both sides because eventually, we want people to retire successfully. longevity is a major issue to all of us. How long will we live? And will we have the resources to continue to live the lifestyle that we're accustomed to?

And that's my specialty, as we call it getting up the mountain, but more importantly, is teaching people how to come down the mountain. Because everyone wants to talk about putting money away, but nobody ever talks about how to take that money out and live an abundance lifestyle. That's where we're our focus is.

Question:

Your typical CPA is just doing tax preparation, whereas you're actually proactively helping guide people.

Joe Yocavitch:

In the beginning of my career, I would clash with CPAs because of how they thought of taxes. But now, we have partnerships. I do business with a lot of CPAs. They think about taxes, in the present. I'm thinking about taxes in the future. CPAs are really good at what they do, there's no question.

But they're dealing with so much information because the tax laws are changing. And they constantly change in retirement. And when I started to partner up with them some years ago, it was amazing how we both worked in conjunction with each other. But more importantly, they're now convinced that my philosophy is now holding up where taxes are going up. I have no control over that because the government constantly changes the game on us. And because of that, we need to be nimble enough to be able to adapt ourselves, to be able to change. And the accountants working with me are changing with that philosophy. So, they become actually more proactive than reactive.

Question:

You've been doing this for 37 years. What's changed from 37 years ago to today? How are things similar? How are things different? What should people be aware of?

Joe Yocavitch:

The biggest concern for me and for the people now, then it was 37 years ago, no one ever thought that you were going to live to 90 or 100. So that became a real issue moving forward, over the last 20 years, because of technology. We're seeing people that are going into retirement, that are also taking care of their mothers and fathers, because of longevity. People had pension plans 37 years ago, and they didn't really concern themselves with the things we have today and all the types of derivatives and investment choices that we have today.

So, I have to not only stay on top of that, for the benefit of the client, but if you notice, many times, we not only take care of the clients, but we take care of their families and we take care of their children. And now we're taking care of a legacy strategy that we're presenting to the people we're talking to.

So, it encompasses, for me, a lot more of making sure that I know what I'm talking about. I'm well-read, besides writing the books. I'm always in tune with the market and what's happening in our government, to be able to know how these things could affect us. It's really fascinating that I get, "If it wasn't for you, we would not be in this situation."

And, Paul, when you hear that, as many times as I have, it really makes you say to yourself, "I'm doing the right thing by these folks. I'm really helping them," which otherwise they would not get this type of help, because most of the time, they're being sold vehicles or products, and they don't know why they bought the products. So, we actually have a really great relationship with all our clients.

Question:

What are your final thoughts for someone watching this video?

Joe Yocavitch:

My final thoughts are be prepared. If you're serious about working with me, like we are, like sports, you need to have your helmet on. You need to be prepared to come to have this type of conversation. You need to be in a proactive mode to really know that I'm going to be able to help bring clarity and simplicity to your life. I will look at your plan through a microscope, I'm going to dissect some of this stuff. I'm going to make it simple, not complicated, but I'm going to make it, where it's more about strategy planning than it is product planning. And that's really the separation of myself, my firm, and other advisors. I have relationships with the top CPAs in the area and the estate planning attorneys in the area.

So, for us, it's allowing the client to come in. And almost like a doctor, I'm going to do a blood test on you. I'm going to do a urine sample. I'm going to do an EKG, an MRI, to make sure you are in perfect health.

If there's something that I see, that concerns me I'm going to address it so you can improve it. Then it's a question of, how do we do that the best way? What's the most efficient way possible to do that? It encompasses a really worthwhile effort on my part to be able to help so many people because we are in a situation that we've never seen before.

And I'm here to tell you, if you're dealing with our firm, the first 15-minute appointment, is basically getting the chance to know you and who you are and what your philosophies are and what your belief system is, and what you've learned in the past and what you believe today, moving forward. But also, how were you affected by the people you worked with, before coming to see me?

That's also important. Did you have a good advisor? Did you have a bad advisor? Did you have someone that's just selling you product, or did you have somebody really taking an in-depth look at how this stuff works, where it benefits you, as opposed to those people?

And that, to me, is the most important thing, and that's what made my business successful. And that's what makes me keep on doing this and waking up every day to try to help as many people as possible.

---

[1]Series 7 license: The Series 7 exam licenses the holder to sell all types of securities products except commodities and futures. Known formally as the General Securities Representative Qualification Examination, the Series 7 exam and its licensing is administered by the Financial Industry Regulatory Authority (FINRA). Stockbrokers in the United States need to pass the Series 7 exam to obtain a license to trade.

[2]The Series 63 is a securities exam and license entitling the holder to solicit orders for any type of security in a particular state. To obtain a Series 63 license, the applicant

must pass an exam and possess knowledge of ethical practices and fiduciary obligations.

[3]Designed by the North American Securities Administrators Association (NASAA) and administered by the Financial Industry Regulatory Authority (FINRA), the Series 65 is an exam and securities license required for individuals to act as investment advisers in the US. The Series 65 exam, known formally as the Uniform Investment Adviser Law Examination, covers laws, regulations, ethics, and various topics important to the role of a financial adviser.

SERVICES

In addition to the ideas and strategies detailed in this book, here is a comprehensive list of the services I offer:

- Financial and Wealth Planning
  - Life Insurance Planning Strategies
  - Buy Sell & Business Insurance
  - Investment Management
  - Kaizen
  - Legacy Planning
  - Results in Advance Planning
  - Retirement Income Planning
  - Roth Conversion Strategies

- Social Security Maximization[1]
- Tax Strategies
- Disability Insurance

You can learn more and get the most up to date information at my website at:
https://jmlfinancialgroup.com/

---

[1]Not associated with or endorsed by the Social Security Administration or any other government agency.

Maximizing your Social Security Benefits assumes foreknowledge of your date of death. If as an example you wait to claim a higher monthly benefit amount but predecease your average life expectancy, it would have been better to claim your benefits at an earlier age with reduced benefits.

—

Disclosures

Securities and Investment Advisory Services offered through Brokers International Financial Services, LLC. member SIPC JML Financial Group and Brokers International Financial Services, LLC. are not affiliated companies.

General Risk Disclosure

Investing in securities involves risk of loss that clients should be prepared to bear. No investment process is free of risk; no strategy or risk management technique can guarantee returns or eliminate risk in any market environment. There is no guarantee that your investment will be profitable. **Past performance is not a guide to future performance.** The value of investments, as well any investment income, is not guaranteed and can fluctuate based on market conditions.

Tax/Legal & IRS Circular 230 Disclosure:

JML Financial Group does not offer legal or tax advice. Please consult the appropriate professional regarding your individual circumstance.

Pursuant to requirements imposed by the Internal Revenue Service, any tax advice contained in this communication (including any attachments) is not intended to be used, and cannot be used, for purposes of avoiding penalties imposed under the United States Internal Revenue Code or promoting, marketing or recommending to another person any tax-related matter. Please contact us if you wish to have formal written advice on this matter.

Made in the USA
Middletown, DE
27 March 2023

27766844R00056